Holistic Interpretation of Autism

HOLISTIC INTERPRETATION OF AUTISM

A Theoretical Framework

Cheryl D. Seifert

UNIVERSITY
PRESS OF
AMERICA

Lanham • New York • London

Copyright © 1990 by
Cheryl D. Seifert

University Press of America®, Inc.
4720 Boston Way
Lanham, Maryland 20706

3 Henrietta Street
London WC2E 8LU England

All rights reserved
Printed in the United States of America
British Cataloging in Publication Information Available

Library of Congress Cataloging-in-Publication Data

Seifert, Cheryl D.
Holistic interpretation of autism : a theoretical framework /
Cheryl D. Seifert.
p. cm.
Includes bibliographical references.
1. Autism—Physiological aspects. 2. Autism—Environmental aspects.
3. Draw-a-person test. I. Title.
RJ506.A9S432   1990   616.89'82—dc20   89–77072 CIP

ISBN 0–8191–7739–3 (alk. paper)
ISBN 0–8191–7740–7 (pbk. : alk. paper)

 The paper used in this publication meets the minimum requirements of American National Standard for Information Sciences—Permanence of Paper for Printed Library Materials, ANSI Z39.48–1984.

To Theodore C. Seifert, Jr.
and
Eleanore S. Seifert

Contents

1. Theoretical Framework for the Study of Autism   1
2. Psychodiagnostic Use of Human-Figure Drawing   7
3. A Biosocial Approach to Personality Assessment   23
   References   71

1

Theoretical Framework for the Study of Autism

INTRODUCTION

There is a tragic disorder known as infantile autism, in which children form a protective shield of nonresponsiveness around themselves. Although parents may inadvertently promote its development, autism stems from the inborn nature of the child (Rimland 1964). Given the occurrence (about 10% [Rimland 1978]) of idiot savants among the autistic, one might hypothesize that autism is part of the "genetic load," a price paid by the population for obtaining some rare form of intelligence.

My mentor in the study of autism was Daniel G. Freedman (1974), a great scholar and sociobiologist. Both he and his teacher, the neurologist Kurt Goldstein (1940), shared a holistic approach to the study of human behavior, which insists that all behavior be considered in its full biological context. It follows that genetics and its laws of segregation and independent assortment must be included in any modern consideration of individual differences in either biological structure or behavior. A holistic study of autism starts with the premise that a combined etiology, comprising biological (genetic variation) and environmental (stress) factors, induces autistic aberration during the entire course of affect development. Biology and culture are neither opposed to nor separate from whatever initiates autistic behavior.

The following sections present a theoretical framework for the study of autism, intended for the graduate student in psychology, special education, and research. (For a historical review of the subject see *Theories of Autism* [Seifert 1990a].) For clarity's sake, I have expressed my clinical speculations in terms of etiology, behavior, and treatment. (For an in-depth description see *Case Studies in Autism: A Young Child and Two Adolescents* [Seifert 1990b].)

ETIOLOGY

Autism is the sign of a primary organic lesion in the central nervous system, in which withdrawal and affectlessness are a protective, secondary mechanism—a result rather than a cause.

In the autistic child's development a pattern of damage to the central nervous system occurs at some critical point. This damage is not typical of anoxia or any known intrauterine infectious disease (such as congenital rubella syndrome) in which more motor deficits are present.

The evidence (Kanner 1949, 1954) that autism appears to occur in highly intelligent parental pairs may not reflect a purely genetic cause, but a biochemical influence or an intrauterine injury. One wonders about autism cases that are not being noticed in less aware and less educated groups. School screening may eventually bear out the suspicion that there are varying degrees and different subclasses of autism.

BEHAVIOR

Biosocial Behavior

Autistic children are in a constant state of hyperstimulation and low sensitivity threshold vis-à-vis all environmental contact; correlated with this are stereotyped activities intended to ward off further external stimulation. A quantitative, hierarchical description of symptoms may reflect the degree of anatomic involvement in combination with environmental stress factors.

Autistic children are an easily traumatized population, a reaction typical of those with organic disorders in which there is a hierarchy of stress symptoms. Even in a wholly compatible environment there will always be symptoms of trauma; there may be fewer of them, but no environment will erase all symptoms.

Adaptive and appropriate behavior in autistic children is not directly comparable with the degree of organic pathology, as demonstrated in a series of longitudinal studies (Seifert 1990b).

Autistic children, on the whole, are low-level functioning individuals, as shown in a cross-sectional study (see Chapter 2).

Affective Behavior

In the affect of autistic children some control mechanism has gone awry. The primary problem is affect expression (mobilization) and control; certain situations have "high arousal energy" and can produce affect in the absence of an adequate cognitive response.

The sequence in which affect development and social responsiveness appear in autistic children is the same as in normal children, but with varyingly delayed onset, with sudden spurts and long plateaus involving more intense and irregular sensitive periods.

Cognitive Behavior

Cognitive deficits in language and nonlanguage behavior vary widely from child to child, reflecting bilateral hemispheric pathology. These deficits seriously limit the development and acquisition of social meaning (inner verbal language and nonverbal social gestures).

The root of the autistic problem may lie not in the failure to acquire language but in the lack of prerequisites for developing a representational system—defined as the ability to represent something by means of a differentiated signifier that serves only a representative purpose, i.e., inner verbal language, mental image, symbolic gesture (Piaget and Inhelder [1966] 1969).

The difficulties faced by autistic children may result from an absence of representational functions, such that the consequences of this deficit represent the syndrome and create the language problems.

Assuming that language is based on the capacity for and final acquisition of a representational system, in defining autistic children we ought to look first at the total representational process rather than language ability alone.

According to Piaget's ([1947] 1950, [1936] 1952, [1937] 1954) hierarchy of cognitive development, at each level of intellectual growth autistic children have such difficulty that it is very unlikely they will reach the formal representational level of cognition. At most, they are able to form associations between events, but have difficulty classifying and categorizing them. Unable to establish meaningful relationships between experiences, they rely on associations among casual similarities. Consequently the surroundings of autistic children lack meaningful structure and their attention jumps from association to association with no real direction.

The absence of adequate representational functions binds autistic children to concreteness (an impairment of the abstract attitude), to the immediate, to that which is displayed in front of them.

Undeveloped representational functions also serve to exacerbate the autistic child's asocial deviation.

Because of the lack of representational functions, autism and central aphasia are easily cross-diagnosed due to similarities in their verbal output.

Affective-Cognitive Behavior

The parallel between affective-cognitive symbiosis and physical maturation manifests in autism as a consequence of the sudden, integrated spurt in affect and cognitive development at 5½ years of age, when traits typical of the infantile autism syndrome gradually modify and autistic children begin to follow paths uniquely their own.

Affect and intelligence interact, cognition serving to control affect and cope with environmental stimulation. Two cardinal points become evident in autism:

1. During early infancy, physiological prototypes of behavioral organization give way to psychophysiological processes as cognition fails to "clock in" at some critical period. A condition of hyperstimulation occurs in which protective withdrawal and depressed affect appear as secondary consequences. Not until after the first year does the autistic child show changes in sensitivity to stimulation and consequent pathological behavior, i.e., being incapable of seeking, maintaining, controlling, and tolerating contact with stimulation.
2. Conversely, a normal reduction in uncontrolled acute fear may be the result of increased cognitive control after age 5½ years (Rimland 1968).

Because the therapist is concerned with diagnosing the autistic condition and with achieving the child's socialization, she or he may fail to observe the timing and patterning of intellectual and affect development, the child's extremely sensitive periods, and low threshold for environmental interactions. (See Chapters 2 and 3 for discussion of human-figure drawing as a psychodiagnostic tool.)

TREATMENT

Autistic behavior may be prematurely labeled "bizarre"—which in some cases it does become—and be aggravated by social factors at critical "turning points" (Erikson 1963), moments of decision between progress and regression, integration and retardation. A four-year therapeutic relationship (Seifert 1990b) that I had with an autistic child led to improved interaction, overall positive response, and a pleasant, fruitful enterprise. This finding supports the conclusion that organicity does not exclude the benefits of psychotherapy, although a high IQ facilitates treatment and improvement. Effective psychotherapy does not depend on viewing the environment as the primary source of pathology.

2

Psychodiagnostic Use of Human-Figure Drawing

Of the many standardized intelligence tests, human-figure drawing (Goodenough 1926) is perhaps the most unusual for its conception, brevity, and general convenience. While still a relatively new tool in assessing intelligence and personality, human-figure drawing has been widely used to study children with hearing handicaps and suspected neurological deficiencies. Human-figure drawing can also reveal and explicate autism. The test requires no sophisticated measuring device or procedure; only one directive needs to be communicated, and the respondent needs little verbal understanding. Designed around a concept that pertains to people in all cultures—the perception and conceptualization of human form—the human-figure drawing test is widely usable as a cross-cultural research instrument.

In research with infants and young children it is possible to assure comparability by (1) making the test situation understandable without verbal explanation, (2) presenting a test problem that invites action, and (3) interpreting the child's response in terms of his or her action. Human-figure drawing, a psychomotor test, complies with all three criteria.

In cross-cultural studies of sensorimotor development in infants, psychologists with an evolutionary perspective such as Freedman (1974) and Scarr-Salapatek (1976) have argued that sensorimotor skills evolved earlier in our primate past than other forms of intelligence, that they are phenotypically less variable because they have been subjected to longer and stronger selection, and that their development is governed both by genetic and developmental adaptation to physical and caretaking environments.

The overall pattern of sensorimotor development appears quite homogeneous for our species, since criterion performance is accomplished for the vast majority of human infants in the first 15 to 20 months. The evidence from cross-cultural studies suggests, however, that the rates of infant development vary among groups and that the origins of these variances are probably partly genetic and possibly partly cultural (Munroe and Munroe 1975; Rebelsky and Daniel 1976).

In addition to being an index of intellectual maturity (Harris 1963; Koppitz 1968), personality, too, is revealed in human-figure drawing. The projective interpretation of personality (Machover 1949; Buck 1948) relies on the presence of specific body parts in the human figure, especially qualitative and symbolic features, for example, the way a part is depicted, relative proportions of parts, treatment of line, contour and shading, expression and "look" of the facial countenance. Unlike the use of human-figure drawing as an index of intellectual maturity, scored by systematic accumulation of points in a scale, its use in assessing personality depends on subjectively judging the effects of graphic elements and their interrelationships. Swensen (1968), in a review of the literature, notes the lack of objectivity and reliability in scoring systems, such as Machover's traditional scoring system (1949), whether based on content or structural variables.

However, Swensen (1968) also indicates one area in which data are promising: the measurement of sex differentiation (Swensen 1955). Global ratings of human-figure drawing have been found (Strumpfer 1963) to achieve levels of reliability in this measurement that, generally, would be considered satisfactory for psychometric purposes.

When I considered using human-figure drawing as an explication of affect expression in autistic children, I explored the Elkisch (1945) method of interpreting children's drawings. (See *Theories of Autism* [Seifert 1990a].) Following Prinzhorn (1923) and Klages (1923), Elkisch established the criteria of rhythm and rule, complexity and simplicity, expansion and compression, integration and disintegration, and realism and symbolism. The strength of these criteria lies in their inclusion of fundamental biological elements of human expression inherent in the movement of line. Analyzing drawings by these criteria reveals the emotional and intellectual attitudes underlying the child's depiction of expressive movements, spatial relationships, and inner experiences. However, as an analytic tool that focuses on the individual, as psychoanalysis also does, these criteria are necessarily limited; the broader, populationwide concepts of modern biology lie outside their scope.

Said another way, since biological principles usually are concerned with populations, a biosocial approach reverses psychology's focus on the individual and views him or her as part of evolutionary processes. Individual behavior or personality is seen (Freedman 1979) as a unique variation on the species' theme, the species' theme being the primary motif. Thus, when future researchers study personality in children's human-figure drawings, they would be well advised to take an "approach from above," or evolutionary view, that starts with whole, naturally occurring phenomena. If one studies infants, start by looking at mothers and their babies in their customary setting, not in the laboratory. In terms of their scope, power, and intellectual appeal, hypotheses derived from evolutionary thinking have no equal.

Once extensive data on human-figure drawing are collected within a culture, a logical second step would be to trace lines of development cross-sectionally to see how affect expression, an adapted behavior and one aspect of the formation of social attachment, becomes part of the societal pattern. Such research can help us see the differences and commonalities in human development. The differences, if seen as adaptive, enlarge our perspective and our understanding of what is normal. Such understanding could provide the missing link in a series of studies (*Theories of Autism* [Seifert 1990a] and *Case Studies in Autism: A Young Child and Two Adolescents* [Seifert 1990b]) that suggest the psychobiology of affect and address the problem of affect and social attachment in autistic children. The research challenge is to articulate propositions governing universal adaptive functions and expressions of children's affect.

Thomas and Chess (1977) describe nine general categories of temperamental characteristics that may be transferable to expressions of affect in children's human-figure drawing: activity level, rhythmicity, approach or withdrawal, adaptability, intensity of reaction, threshold of responsiveness, quality of mood, distractibility, and attention and persistence. Along the same lines, in a temperament theory of personality development, Buss and Plomin (1975) define emotionality in terms of arousal, reactivity, and excitability, and discuss temperament adaptivity that may have implications for the study of affect in human-figure drawing. If low affect is maladaptive, does it not fail to meet one of the criteria of affect adaptiveness? Possibly the answer lies in the notion of optimal levels of affect arousal, reactivity, and excitability, with the large mid-range of temperaments being the most adaptive, and the extremes, such as affectlessness in autism, the least adaptive. If affect augments drives, motivations, or cognition, then affectlessness, could lead to less urgency or salience in other processes, including cognition—resulting in lessened problem-solving ability and, in turn, a deficient development of the affective system. Memories and perceptions strongly associated with affect would also be less likely to occur, and this low interaction would be reflected in a deficient learning system.

Research from the field of sociobiology may also be useful in studying affect in children's drawings. Morris (1962), for example, studied the picture-making behavior of chimpanzees and its relationship to human art. From this, he established a set of biologically-based asthetic principles: self-rewarding activation, compositional control, calligraphic differentiation, thematic variation, optimum heterogeneity, and universal imagery.

Examination of the affect unique to our species, to a culture, or to a child possessing a particular predisposition toward affect expression-reception, control, symbolic functioning, or introspection offers fertile ground for future research.

HUMAN-FIGURE DRAWINGS OF 16 AUTISTIC CHILDREN: A PARTIAL STUDY

A computer and manual literature search (August 1989) turned up no documented research on human-figure drawing by autistic children, following the American Psychiatric Association's diagnostic criteria for autism. Sixteen young autistic children were administered the Goodenough Draw-a-Man Test (Goodenough 1926) in 1983. All graded in the lower percentiles (excluding the 5 nonrespondents) and 8 of 11 graded below standard score 70, confirming conclusions from various IQ tests that autistics are extremely limited intellectually, and that this can be established by a procedure not subject to reservations about testing difficulty. The study's chief merit lies in having provided data about autistic children's performance on a human-figure drawing test—information unavailable elsewhere in the literature.

Study Design

Human-figure drawings from 11 of 16 young autistic children is reflected in subjects numbered 1, 2, 3, 5, 7, 9, 10, 11, 12, 13, and 14. They range in age from 3 to 12½ years; 14 are male, 2 female; 1 is European, 4 are Afro-American, and 11 are European-American. (See Table 2-1.) The children were being studied (B. L. Leventhal pers.

Table 2-1
Comparison of IQ Performance of 16 Autistic Children

Number[a]	Age	Cultural Background	Sex	Standard IQ Test Score	Human-Figure Drawing Test Raw Score	Human-Figure Drawing Test Standard Score	Human-Figure Drawing Test Percentile Rank
1	8–6	European-American	M	49	12	73	4
2	10–5	European-American	M	49	0	<50	1
3	11–0	European-American	M	44 ± 3	5	55	1
4[b]	8–0	Afro-American	M	63	0	50	1
5	6–1	European-American	F	47	0	52	1
6[b]	5–9	European-American	M	39	0	53	1
7	6–6	European-American	M	16	0	52	1
8[b]	5–9	Afro-American	M	57	0	53	1
9	8–9	Afro-American	F	39	7	58	1
10	3–9	European-American	M	61	0	68	2
11	10–3	European-American	M	38 ± 3	4	54	1
12	7–5	European	M	45	6	64	1
13	9–3	European-American	M	40	15	74	4
14	12–6	European-American	M	None	21	73	4
15[c]	10–6	Afro-American	M	33 ± 3	0	<50	1
16[b]	3–0	European-American	M	33	0	68	2

[a] The number assigned to a patient during an international study of the effects of fenfluramine on blood serotonin and autistic symptoms.
[b] Subject drew nothing; treated as nonrespondent.
[c] Subject did not draw a human figure and responded only after much coaxing; treated as nonrespondent.

com. February 1983; Ritvo et al. 1986) for the effect of fenfluramine on blood serotonin and symptoms of autism at the University of Chicago Pritzker School of Medicine, one of a series of studies conducted at 23 centers, involving approximately 175 patients. These 16 autistic children were selected from a broader sample of 45 self-selected families (the oldest, 22 years) because they were young, had extensive autistic symptoms, and had high levels of serotonin. The autistic children screened included 1 Hispanic-Cuban, 1 Italian, 1 Pole, 15 Afro-Americans, 27 European-Americans, and no Orientals. They were a representative cross-section of the autistic population in the Midwest, with different cultures and varying socioeconomic levels; more than half had low incomes. They had varying degrees of language ability, ranging from some to none. All but two attended special education classes; one exception had recently immigrated from Italy where special education was not available, the other was in residential placement. All subjects in the study clearly fit the criteria of the *Diagnostic and Statistical Manual of Mental Disorders* (American Psychiatric Association 1980) and the National Society for Autistic Children (Ritvo and Freeman 1978).

In this double-blind placebo crossover study, each subject was tested with a standardized IQ test (Wechsler Intelligence Scale for Children-Revised, Cattell Infant Intelligence Scale or Stanford-Binet Intelligence Scale for Children, and Merrill-Palmer Preschool Performance Tests) and a receptive language test. In addition, two independent observers evaluated the subject on each clinic visit according to an observation scale (Freeman et al. 1986). This included observing the subject during breakfast with his family in the hospital cafeteria, during a 10-minute videotape of the subject with a parent or sibling attempting to engage the subject in play, and during a 40-minute videotape of the subject with an inactive adult in a room furnished with selected toys, e.g., crayons and paper, Cootie, medium-sized rubber ball, Crystal Climbers, Bristle Blocks, plastic ring pole, jigsaw puzzle, Bubble Soap, small toy cars, Busy Railroad Set, a top, stuffed doll, plastic glasses, and nose-moustache masks.

Each subject was observed and tested twice in the first month, once per month thereafter for the next 6 months, and in one follow-up clinic visit 3 months after completion of the study. The parents participated in a social history, provided a detailed diary of the subject's home activity, and served as liaison between the study and the school by supplying the subject's teacher(s) with a checklist to be filled out weekly. The subjects were accepted into the study on a contract basis, and, baring illness, the families committed to participate until the study's completion. This multicenter fenfluramine study provides a vast library of data.

Method

The technique for administering human-figure drawing consisted of inducing subjects by gesture and verbal request "to draw a whole person," offering them pencils or crayons and standard-size manilla paper. The specific verbal instructions of the Goodenough Test, to draw "a whole man and the best man you can draw, make *all* of him," were given along with gestures, using the word "boy" with male subjects and "girl" with female subjects.

Subjects were brought to the University of Chicago by their parents from different parts of the Midwest and given several trials at drawing on different days. Better days—those that did not include the routine blood tests that were part of the larger fenfluramine study—were carefully chosen to minimize upsetting influences and give each respondent the benefit of any doubt in evaluating intellectual maturity. Parents were asked to help instigate a drawing when the subject could not or would not grasp the task.

Several subjects drew more than one drawing. The best, most mature drawing was selected and scored. But even such a simple procedure posed difficulties for some. Five subjects did not draw a human figure; one, with assistance from his parent, instead copied a house (No. 15). The remaining 11 subjects (Nos. 1, 2, 3, 5, 7, 9, 10, 11, 12, 13, and 14) attempted some representation, however primitive, of the human figure. From the inclusion of body detail in a number of these drawings, it seems fair to conclude that it is possible to communicate the desired task to autistic children and expect that the drawing rendered can provide a basis for estimating intellectual maturity, even at the lower end of the population norm.

Findings and Observations

Because all of the rendered drawings were quite primitive compared with the scoring criteria designed by Goodenough (1926) and Harris (1963), I elected to do all the scoring myself. I did the scoring twice, with a 3-day interval between gradings and observed only one deviation between the scores, which are presented in Table 2-1.

The sample tested here is, of course, too small to permit any analysis among the various cultural or gender-related demographics, nor was that the intent. Neither should any attempt be made to generalize from these data. But two things might usefully be observed. First, that the correlation between respondent's age and standard score (based only on those respondents with a raw score above zero) is sufficiently low (+ .21) to reduce any concern that the norming of the Goodenough scoring by respondent's age might be biased at the low end of intellectual maturity. Second, considering only the scores of those who can be assumed to have understood the requirement and attempted to comply (i.e., excluding the four nonrespondents and the subject who copied a house), all subjects graded in the lower percentiles and 8 of 11 graded below standard score 70, confirming the results of IQ tests (all of the subjects' IQ scores measured in the lowest 10 percentile and 80% of the subjects graded below IQ 50). This further substantiates that the intellectual level of autistics can be established by a procedure that is independent of language and does not present unidentified testing difficulties.

An in-depth study of an autistic child that combines an ideographic case history with a theoretical perspective is presented in *Case Studies in Autism: A Young Child and Two Adolescents* (Seifert 1990b). In the human-figure drawings of three high-functioning (IQ over 70) autistic children, I observed the difficulty they had in expressing and controlling affect. Most of the time, the autistic children's human-figure drawings showed they had either extreme control over the mobilization of affect or lost control entirely. The two children whose drawings showed the most affect expression remained highly controlled in drawing tasks of their own choosing and, in general, tended not to draw the human figure.

Conclusion

Eleven human-figure drawings from 16 young autistic children were analyzed for their intellectual maturity. The majority of drawings show low-level functioning individuals; other drawings suggest slightly better motor and intellectual functions and areas of strength. However, compared with the drawings of their peers, these indicate capacities far below the normal.

Further, the majority of drawings express affect; some suggest loss of affect control; others suggest more ease of expression and greater control of affect. Eliciting human-figure drawings from autistic children is extremely difficult, since as a group they tend not to draw human figures. This partial study provides human-figure drawings by autistic children that exist nowhere else in the literature. It fills a research gap and suggests the psychodiagnostic significance of such drawing.

Psychodiagnostic Use of Figure Drawing 15

Subject 1. European-American boy; age, 8 yrs, 6 mos.

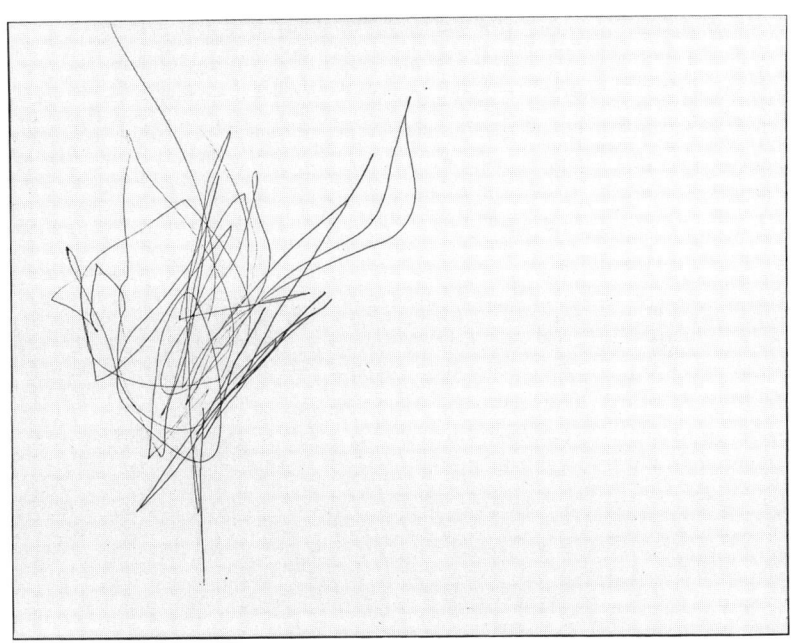

Subject 2. European-American boy; age, 10 yrs, 5 mos.

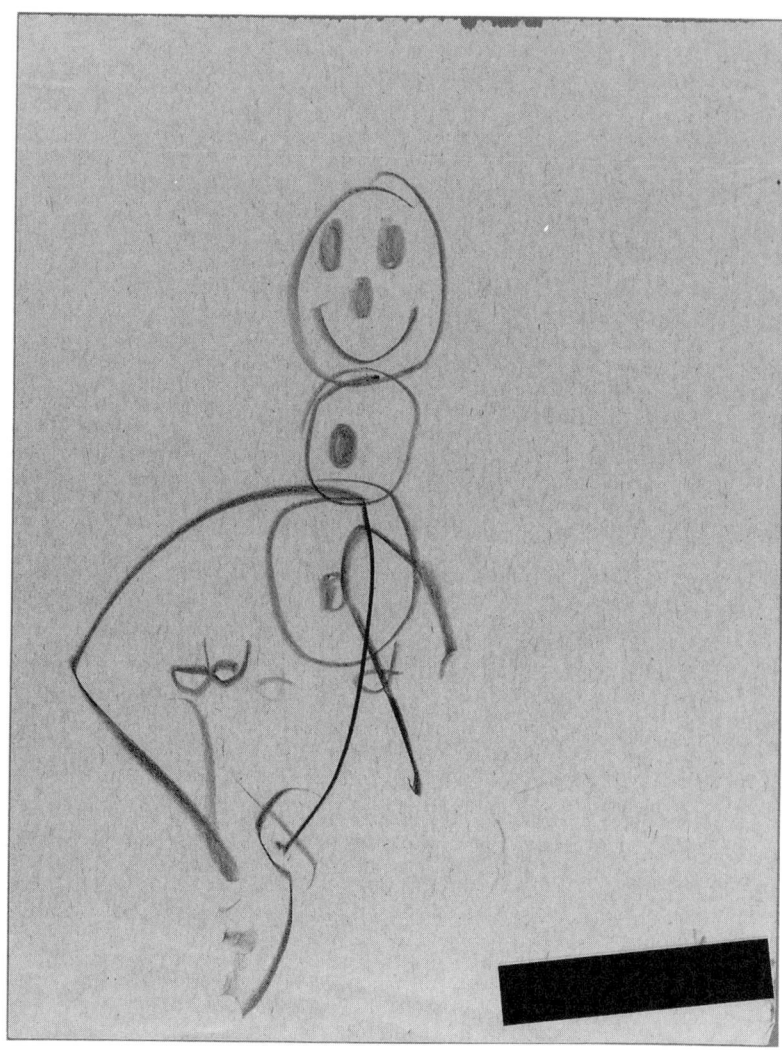

Subject 3. European-American boy; age, 11 yrs.

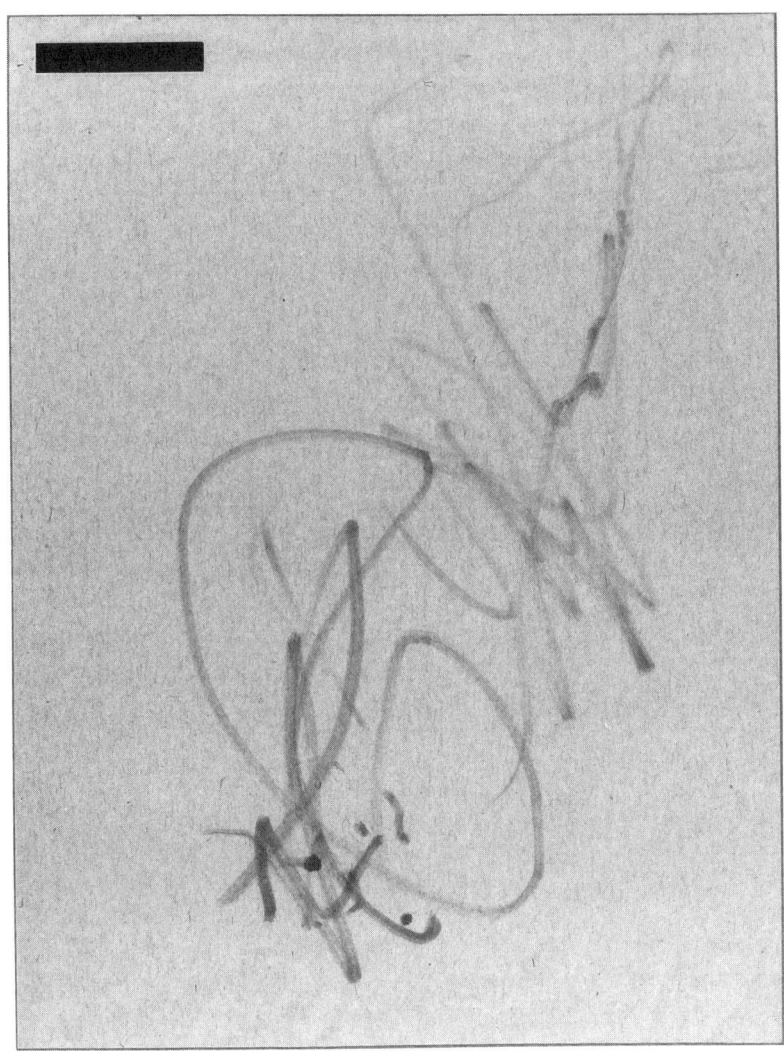

Subject 5. European-American girl; age, 6 yrs, 1 mo.

Subject 7. European-American boy; age, 6 yrs, 6 mos.

Subject 9. Afro-American girl; age, 8 yrs, 9 mos.

Psychodiagnostic Use of Figure Drawing 19

Subject 10. European-American boy; age, 3 yrs, 9 mos.

Subject 11. European-American boy; age, 10 yrs, 3 mos.

Subject 12. European boy; age, 7 yrs, 5 mos.

Subject 13. European-American boy; age, 9 yrs, 3 mos.

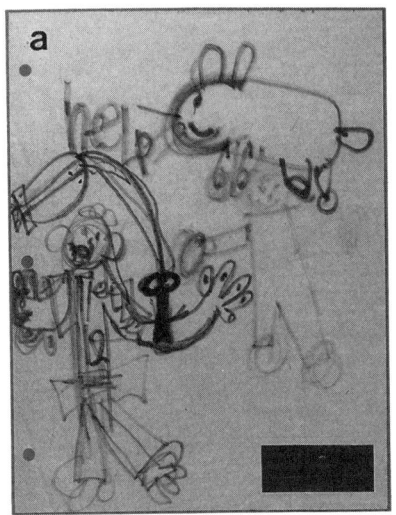 

Subject 14. European-American boy; age, 12 yrs, 6 mos.

3

A Biosocial Approach to Personality Assessment

The hallmark of the biosocial approach to behavior is endeavoring to understand, in an evolutionary context, adaptive functions of human behavior. Since some differences in the biologically adaptive role of the sexes occur in all species, the study of male-female differences is standard biosocial subject matter. Much has been written by psychologists contrasting the behavior of the sexes, but their differences have seldom been considered in an evolutionary context.

For several years I have been interested in affect and mechanisms of social attachment, behavior I view as being phylogenetically adaptive. I presented a study (Seifert 1990a, 1990b) showing that affect occurs in autistic children, but its control mechanism has gone awry.

From an evolutionary point of view, phylogenetically adaptive social signals must be matched by complementary receiving mechanisms. For example, the baby's smile is meaningless without a sympathetic recipient or participant in that smile. Although my mentor, Daniel G. Freedman, stated this 20 years ago (1968a, 1968b; see also *Theories of Autism* [Seifert 1990a] for an in-depth discussion of Freedman's biological approach to personality theory, and Goldstein's [1957] important work), I have recently realized that many evolved behavioral mechanisms in the infant and child have counterpart reactions in the caretaking adult.

For example, crying is a phylogenetically adaptive mechanism; easily within hours after birth and before the first feeding, a crying infant will become quiet when held and carried—a response that coordinates wonderfully with the anxiety felt by the parent until the infant is quieted. In this way, without having the ability to cling, as most newborn mammals do, the human infant gets next to its parent.

Another example of human mutuality is the 2-month-old infant's persistent searching for the face of an adult and the love and closeness a normal adult feels as their eyes meet and the first smiles ensue. An infant smiles most readily at the full face view of an adult; if the profile is turned, the infant's smile disappears (see Kaila 1932). Soon an infant starts to coo at the adult. For an adult to withhold and not coo back feels unnatural. The infant is beginning to "talk" and an adult feels an irresistible urge to respond. Freedman (1968a) purports that it is exactly these kinds of species-specific mutualities that form our early social bonds.

Laughter, which occurs in the infant at about 4 months of age, and the happiness it gives an adult, is another strong bonding behavior. Just before 1-year old, a fear of strangers develops, which also draws the infant and caretaker closer together. By the time the infant begins to imitate words, usually during the first year, secure social bonds have already formed and the child is an important part of those around him.

While the bonding interactions between infants and adults may be self-evident, evolved mechanisms of social interactions are manifest in all aspects of man's behavior. For example, male-male competition seems predicated on the evolution of dominance rivalry widely seen in group-living species. It appears from the studies of Ardrey (1966), Chance and Jolly (1970), and DeVore and Washburn (1963) that man behaves like any other terrestrial primate when it comes to displaying dominance-submission hierarchies. Competitive interplay, the need to win and to be "top dog," is readily seen in young schoolboys (Freedman 1975), as it is in young baboons and macaques (DeVore and Washburn 1963). Freedman (1975, 1976) described boys of 3 and 4 years old already vying with one another. When male 4-year-olds were paired and asked "Which of you is toughest?" both partners in 60% of pairs answered, "Me!" By 6 years of age, however, the same pairs of boys tended to agree that one or the other was toughest, and a clear-cut hierarchy (known as a "pecking order" in chickens) was seen in every classroom studied. Commonly, 80% agreement was found among children when ranking the entire class on toughness (Omark and Edelman 1973). In other words, there is an "attention structure" in primate hierarchies, with attention invariably focused on the most powerful.

Freedman (1975) noted another male tendency that emerged from these studies: males tend to rank themselves higher than others generally rank them. This "overrating" phenomenon, is similar to the behavior he found in the 4-year-old boys who each insisted he was toughest.

Girls, however, are not as emotionally involved in ranking themselves. Freedman (1975) found that girls agreed they would like to be known as the "nicest," however, they never developed a competitive ranking of themselves regarding this trait. At a very early age, boys and girls exhibit decidedly different social strategies, with boys more aggressively competitive and girls more oriented toward social networks, relationships, and friendships (Stevens 1972).

The same patterns of boy-girl differences in play behavior, familiar from United States and Afro-American observations, have been noted (Freedman 1974, 1976) in cross-cultural data on the play of 5- to 7-year-olds in Japan, Hong Kong, Bali, Sri Lanka, India, Kenya, and among Australian Aborigines and Navajo Indians. In each of these groups, boys were more aggressive with one another, ran in larger groups, and covered more physical space. Girls tended to hold more conversations with their nearest neighbor and engaged in more activities involving repeated movement or patterns; boys tended toward physical interactions and less predictable activities. The cross-cultural continuities, based on extensive notes, were substantial (Freedman 1976, percentages not cited).

There seems little doubt that humans follow the primate tradition of displaying somewhat higher male exploratory and female affiliative behavior, high inter-male competition, and a male tendency to group together into a dominance-submission hierarchy.

To define units of human behavior meaningful for study, one has to think in evolutionary terms. For the personality theorist an evolutionary view leads to the realization that people often act unconsciously in mutual concert and are built to send and receive cues in the service of certain evolved behavior. It requires some ingenuity to identify the common units of evolved behavior and devise an appropriate test. The following ongoing study aims to establish a universally applicable test for the study of affect.

AFFECT IN THE HUMAN-FIGURE DRAWINGS OF CHINESE AND AFRO-AMERICAN CHILDREN

Research Aim and Significance

The aim of this study is to describe and compare affect expression in two groups of children, Chinese and Afro-American. A group of existing studies demonstrated growing evidence that cross-culturally consistent sex differences reflect psychobiological differences (Erikson 1975; Freedman 1968b, 1974, 1976; Freedman and Freedman 1969; Garai and Scheinfeld 1968; Lewis et al. 1966; McLean 1970; Omark et al. 1975). These studies, involving the behavior of newborns and schoolchildren, have found significant social and emotional differences between the sexes. Consideration of these findings instigated the following study of affect differences in the human-figure drawings of Chinese and Afro-American boys and girls.

Figures 3-1 through 3-71 were selected from among 260 drawings and are presented as a cross-cultural reference in which sexually differentiated emotional expression probably reflects psychobiological differences. Such cultural comparisons can also shed light on affect as a social lubricant and a biological mechanism whereby social relationships are fostered. Most current knowledge of optimal affect expression comes from research on Caucasian subjects. Consequently, many investigators of child development have acquired a limited view of normal affective processes in a pluralistic, biologically diverse population such as ours.

A second goal of this study is to identify the cultural variations found in human-figure drawing that are central to affect expression and healthy social relationships. Understanding the potential range of normal, adaptive affect can also help avoid unwarranted and detrimental clinical interventions.

Method

The groups studied consisted of 110 Chinese children, Hong Kong born, and mostly of Cantonese background, chosen from a group of schoolchildren in Chicago's Chinese community, and 150 Afro-American children, United States born, from a group of Chicago inner-city schoolchildren. They were grouped in matched ages ranging from 4 to 5, 8 to 9, and 13 to 14 years old. The human-figure drawing test was administered to elicit affect comparisons of sex differences between the two groups.

Since many of the Chinese had been in the United States less than 6 months, and more than 50% of them did not speak English, drawings were obtained through translated instructions of "draw a person."

Findings and Observations

Table 3-1 represents an analysis of human-figure drawings from both groups. In a broad comparison of human-figure drawings by boys

Table 3-1
Sex Differences in Two Cultures: Comparative Percentages of Differentiating Categories Displayed in Human-Figure Drawings

	Sex	Chinese (Ages 4-5)	Chinese (Ages 8-9)	Chinese (Ages 13-14)	Afro-American (Ages 4-5)	Afro-American (Ages 8-9)	Afro-American (Ages 13-14)
Vehicles	M	66.7*	5.0	0.0	0.0	8.8	4.5
	F	0.0	0.0	0.0	0.0	0.0	0.0
Flowers	M	50.0	0.0*	0.0	4.8	0.0*	0.0
	F	20.0	25.0	11.1	5.5	17.1	5.0
Hero's role, portrayed as competitor, warrior, and physical strongman	M	0.0	35.0*	35.7*	0.0	38.2*	36.4*
	F	0.0	0.0	0.0	0.0	2.8	5.0
Movement**	M	66.7	35.0	50.0	9.5	64.7	72.7*
	F	20.0	14.3	27.8	11.1	34.3	25.0
Male figures	M	66.7*	100.0*	96.4*	95.2*	100.0*	100.0*
	F	0.0	0.0	5.5	5.5	0.0	0.0
Female figures	M	0.0*	0.0*	0.0*	4.8*	0.0*	0.0*
	F	90.0	100.0	100.0	88.9	100.0	100.0
Number of subjects	M	6	20	28	21	34	22
	F	10	28	18	18	35	20

*$p < .05$.
**Representation can include a vehicle or object having the potential for movement, a figure's raised limb, a line connecting objects, repeated lines in any direction.

and girls, boys in both cultures drew more male figures and girls more female figures (Figs. 3-1 through 3-71). This may be a projection of the self, or reflect the tendency for children to seek out and play with others of the same sex. Both boys and girls spontaneously accompanied their human-figure drawings with accessories and objects, although the only instruction was to draw a figure. Girls in all age groups included flowers (Figs. 3-16, 3-17, 3-33, 3-36, 3-41, 3-54, 3-55, and 3-69) in their human-figure drawings; boys, age group 4 to 5, also included flowers, along with vehicles such as trains, cars, and trucks (Figs. 3-1, 3-2, and 3-40).

Boys, ages 8 to 9 and 13 to 14 years old, in both cultures conveyed motion (Figs. 3-11, 3-24, 3-46, 3-60, 3-61, and 3-62) by such means as a line drawn from a figure to a car to indicate the figure going to the car, by drawing a raised limb, or by many lines spiraling across the drawing. Girls in the same age group, drew more stationary figures (Figs. 3-5, 3-34, 3-38, 3-39, 3-56, and 3-57). Same-age boys, ages 8 years and older, assumed a hero's role in their drawings, as winners of sports competitions, warriors, and exemplars of physical strength (Figs. 3-7, 3-8, 3-46, 3-48, 3-64, and 3-65). Girls, on the other hand, at none of these ages showed competitive ranking of themselves.

In addition to consistent cross-cultural differences between the sexes, differences were evident in the way boys and girls in each culture expressed affect. Fairytale themes and mythology predominated in the drawings of Chinese boys and girls, whereas everyday activities were common in drawings of the Afro-Americans. With controlled drawing, Chinese boys, 8 to 9 and 13 to 14 years old, made accurate representations of heroes competing in the guise of mythical and religious characters. They portrayed soldiers at war, captains with weapons and medals, and kings with crowns (Figs. 3-6 and 3-23). The same-age Afro-American boys more often assumed the hero's role as musclemen, bursting with action (Fig. 3-61), and as killers and gangsters armed with guns and knives (Figs. 3-42 and 3-44).

Chinese girls, 8 to 9 and 13 to 14 years old, exhibited femaleness by drawing comely, restrained, princesslike figures, typically fairy queens or royal personages with ornate or peasant costumes in peaceful landscapes (Figs. 3-17, 3-19, 3-35, and 3-36). Afro-American girls exhibited femaleness in highly sexualized figures, with accentuated eyelashes and lips, shapely bodies, and "bustiness" (Figs. 3-55, 3-66, and 3-70). Their figures were commonly in recreational settings such as at play, dancing, and at the beach.

Another finding from this study is that Chinese children in all age groups exhibited in their drawings a placid, accommodating attitude. The emotional expression of their human figures was consistently highly controlled, conveying a sense of restraint or impassivity. The same-age Afro-Americans showed figures with strong affect and extremes of affect.

While being administered the test, Chinese children behaved thoughtfully and studiously as a group; Afro-Americans impulsively acted out their feelings. In contrast to their outwardly restrained appearance, young 4- to 5-year-old Chinese children were very actively engaged in creating their drawings (Fig. 3-1). Young Chinese drawers included geometric patterns and colors, appeared cognitively quick, motorically adept, and developmentally advanced (Figs. 3-3 and 3-4). In comparison, 4- to 5-year-old Afro-American children drew quite simple, barely embellished drawings (Fig. 3-40). Chinese drawers, ages 8 to 9, frequently utilized rulers and drew exact, carefully articulated pictures (Figs. 3-14 and 3-15). Afro-American drawers of the same age drew imprecisely and with gross approximations (Fig. 3-49).

Conclusion

My conclusion, which is compatible with Freedman's (1976), is that it seems likely these cross-culturally consistent sex differences reflect psychobiological differences. This finding may support a psychobiological explanation of the differences in affect observable in autistic children. When Garai and Scheinfeld (1968) claim that males everywhere exhibit greater attraction to and interest in the display of aggression, when Freedman (1968b) finds little boys less passive, more negativistic, more aggressive, more rivalrous, or more investigative than little girls, and when Mead (1939) notes that it is the tendency for young males everywhere to travel farther from the home, they may well be speaking of biologically-based tendencies that also underlie the differences we perceive in their play constructions and drawings.

As a final point, I would like to offer Freedman's (Freedman, Loring, and Martin 1967, p. 470) definition of personality: "a Gestalt array of species traits, usually related to interpersonal behavior, which vary uniquely for each individual because the genotype is unique, the individual experience is unique, and the interaction between genotype and experience is unique." The fresh aspect of Freedman's definition is that it brings the species concept to the fore and thereby provides a structure in which all hominids may be compared according to their unique variation on the hominid theme. In the words of Freedman (1968b, p. 259), "this emphasis on evolved behavior is not meant to deny that familial and cultural institutions do indeed differentially influence behavior and personality. We will rather, emphasize that such institutions only support or shape man's behavior and do not create it, as it were, out of the blue."

In a unique study of ethnic differences in emotional expression, Freedman and Freedman (1969) observed behavioral differences as early as the second day of life. American newborns were found to be significantly more excitable and labile in affect than were Chinese newborns. These ethnic differences are surely inherited, for there is no way they could have been acquired so early in life. The only reasonable explanation must be that "While it must be true that different cultural practices differentially reward babies' behavior, it is equally likely that biological predispositions affect what become the cultural norms" (Freedman 1971, p. 228).

Personality Assessment 31

Figure 3-1. Chinese boy, age group 4 to 5 years old.

Figure 3-2. Chinese boy, age group 4 to 5 years old.

Figure 3-3. Chinese boy, age group 4 to 5 years old. Free drawing.

Figure 3-4. Chinese girl, age group 4 to 5 years old.

Figure 3-5. Chinese girl, age group 4 to 5 years old.

Personality Assessment 35

Figure 3-6. Chinese boy, age group 8 to 9 years old.

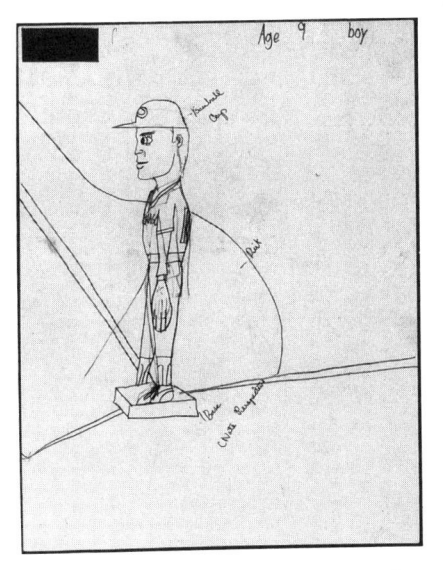

Figure 3-7. Chinese boy, age group 8 to 9 years old.

Figure 3-8. Chinese boy, age group 8 to 9 years old.

Figure 3-9. Chinese boy, age group 8 to 9 years old.

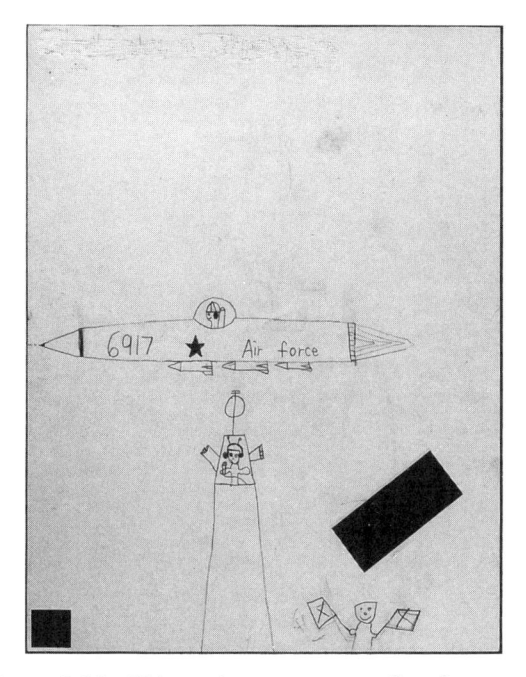

Figure 3-10. Chinese boy, age group 8 to 9 years old.

Figure 3-11. Chinese boy, age group 8 to 9 years old.

38 Autism

Figure 3-12. Chinese boy, age group 8 to 9 years old. Free drawing.

Figure 3-13. Chinese boy, age group 8 to 9 years old. Free drawing.

Personality Assessment 39

Figure 3-14. Chinese boy, age group 8 to 9 years old. Free drawing.

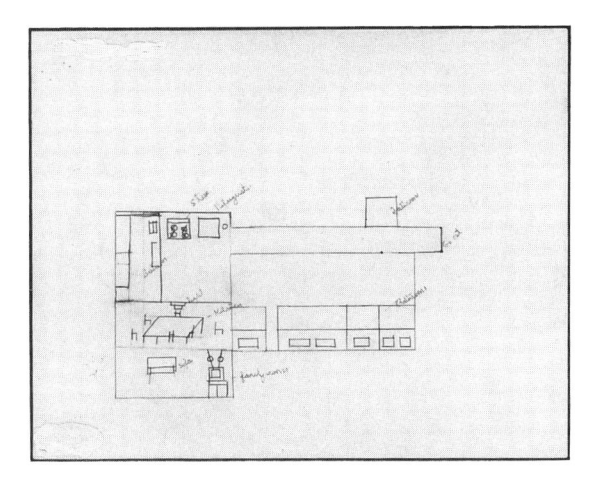

Figure 3-15. Chinese boy, age group 8 to 9 years old. House.

40   Autism

Figure 3-16. Chinese girl, age group 8 to 9 years old.

Figure 3-17. Chinese girl, age group 8 to 9 years old.

Figure 3-18. Chinese girl, age group 8 to 9 years old.

Figure 3-19. Chinese girl, age group 8 to 9 years old.

42   Autism

Figure 3-20. Chinese girl, age group 8 to 9 years old. Free drawing.

Figure 3-21. Chinese girl, age group 8 to 9 years old. Free drawing.

Personality Assessment 43

Figure 3-22. Chinese boy, age group 13 to 14 years old.

Figure 3-23. Chinese boy, age group 13 to 14 years old.

44   Autism

Figure 3-24. Chinese boy, age group 13 to 14 years old.

Figure 3-25. Chinese boy, age group 13 to 14 years old.

Personality Assessment 45

Figure 3-26. Chinese boy, age group 13 to 14 years old.

Figure 3-27. Chinese boys, age group 13 to 14 years old.

Figure 3-28. Chinese boy, age group 13 to 14 years old.

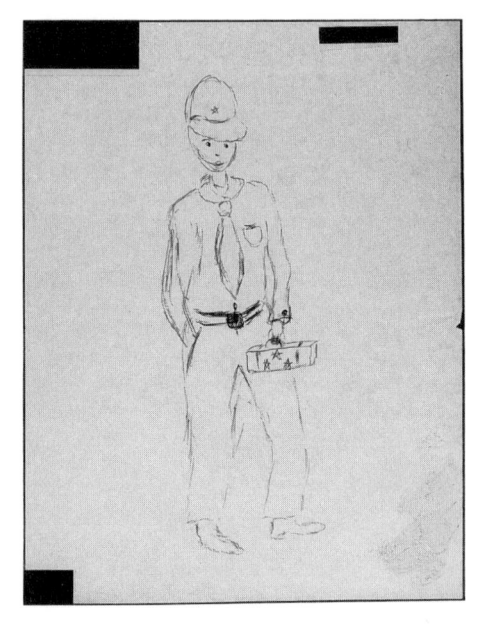

Figure 3-29. Chinese boy, age group 13 to 14 years old.

Figure 3-30. Chinese boy, age group 13 to 14 years old.

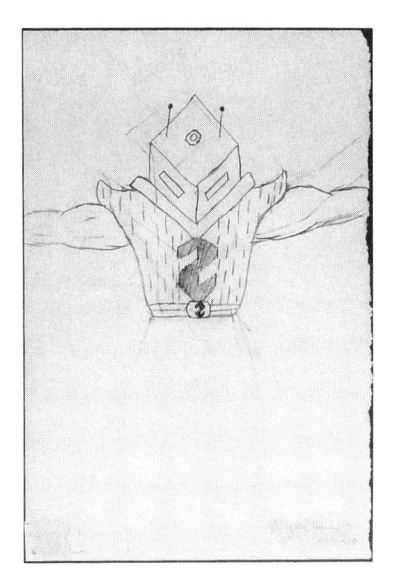

Figure 3-31. Chinese boy, age group 13 to 14 years old.

Figure 3-32. Chinese girl, age group 13 to 14 years old.

Figure 3-33. Chinese girl, age group 13 to 14 years old.

Personality Assessment 49

Figure 3-34. Chinese girl, age group 13 to 14 years old.

Figure 3-35. Chinese girl, age group 13 to 14 years old.

Figure 3-36. Chinese girl, age group 13 to 14 years old.

Figure 3-37. Chinese girl, age group 13 to 14 years old.

Personality Assessment 51

Figure 3-38. Chinese girl, age group 13 to 14 years old.

Figure 3-39. Chinese girl, age group 13 to 14 years old.

Figure 3-40. Afro-American boys, age group 4 to 5 years old.

Personality Assessment 53

Figure 3-41. Afro-American girls, age group 4 to 5 years old.

54   Autism

Figure 3-42. Afro-American boy, age group 8 to 9 years old.

Figure 3-43. Afro-American boy, age group 8 to 9 years old.

Figure 3-44. Afro-American boy, age group 8 to 9 years old.

Figure 3-45. Afro-American boy, age group 8 to 9 years old.

Figure 3-46. Afro-American boy, age group 8 to 9 years old.

Personality Assessment 57

Figure 3-47. Afro-American boy, age group 8 to 9 years old.

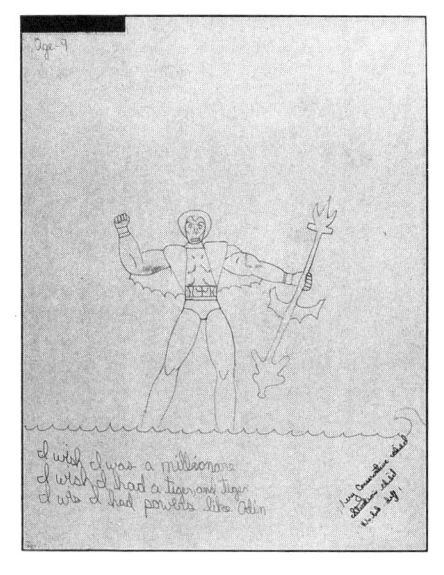

Figure 3-48. Afro-American boy, age group 8 to 9 years old.

Figure 3-49. Afro-American boy, age group 8 to 9 years old. Free drawing.

Personality Assessment 59

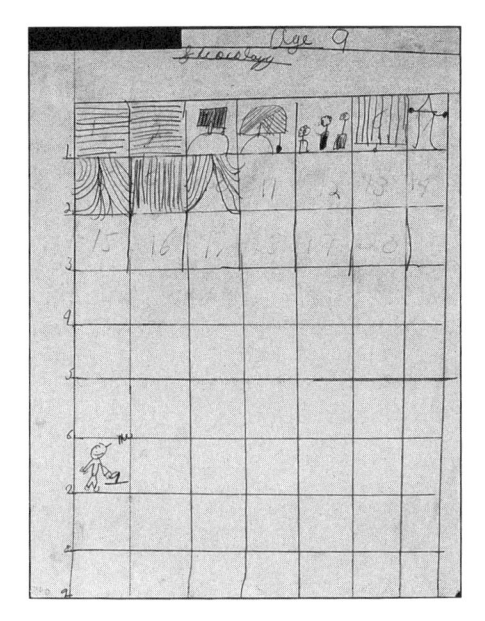

Figure 3-50. Afro-American boy, age group 8 to 9 years old. House.

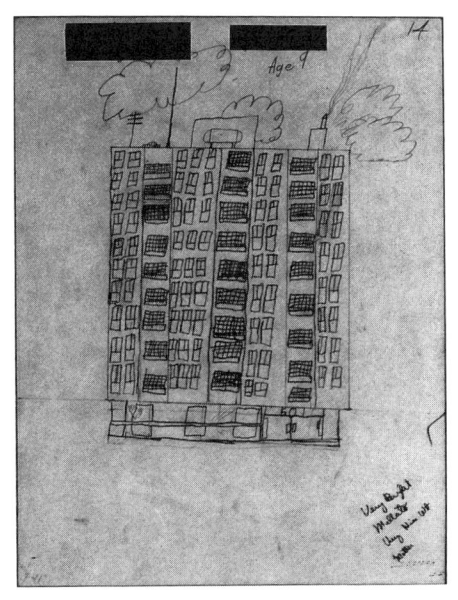

Figure 3-51. Afro-American boy, age group 8 to 9 years old. House.

Figure 3-52. Afro-American girl, age group 8 to 9 years old.

Figure 3-53. Afro-American girl, age group 8 to 9 years old.

Personality Assessment 61

Figure 3-54. Afro-American girl, age group 8 to 9 years old.

Figure 3-55. Afro-American girl, age group 8 to 9 years old.

Figure 3-56. Afro-American girl, age group 8 to 9 years old.

Figure 3-57. Afro-American girl, age group 8 to 9 years old.

Figure 3-58. Afro-American boy, age group 13 to 14 years old.

Figure 3-59. Afro-American boy, age group 13 to 14 years old.

Figure 3-60. Afro-American boy, age group 13 to 14 years old.

Figure 3-61. Afro-American boy, age group 13 to 14 years old.

Personality Assessment

Figure 3-62. Afro-American boy, age group 13 to 14 years old.

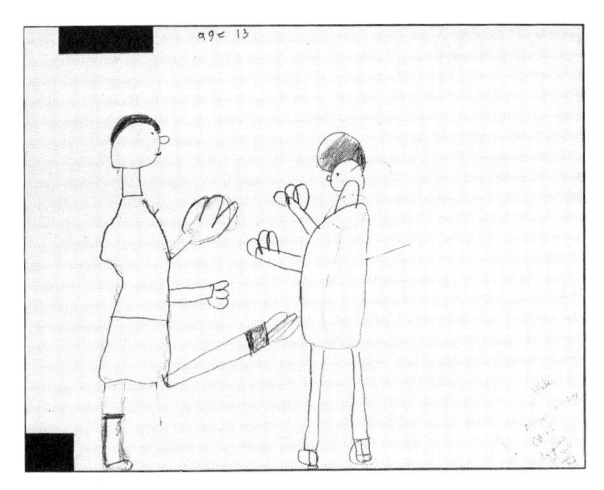

Figure 3-63. Afro-American boy, age group 13 to 14 years old.

Figure 3-64. Afro-American boy, age group 13 to 14 years old.

Figure 3-65. Afro-American boy, age group 13 to 14 years old.

Personality Assessment 67

Figure 3-66. Afro-American girl, age group 13 to 14 years old.

Figure 3-67. Afro-American girl, age group 13 to 14 years old.

68 Autism

Figure 3-68. Afro-American girl, age group 13 to 14 years old.

Figure 3-69. Afro-American girl, age group 13 to 14 years old.

Figure 3-70. Afro-American girl, age group 13 to 14 years old.

Figure 3-71. Afro-American girl, age group 13 to 14 years old.

References

American Psychiatric Association 1980. *Diagnostic and Statistical Manual of Mental Disorders.* 3rd ed. Washington: American Psychiatric Association.

Ardrey, R. 1966. *The Territorial Imperative: A Personal Inquiry into the Animal Origins of Property and Nations.* New York: Atheneum.

Buck, J. N. 1948. The H-T-P technique; a qualitative scoring manual. *Journal of Clinical Psychology* 4:317–96.

Buss, A. H., and Plomin, R. 1975. *A Temperament Theory of Personality Development.* New York: Wiley.

Chance, M., and Jolly, C. J. 1970. *Societies of Monkeys, Apes, and Men.* New York: Dutton.

DeVore, I., and Washburn, S. 1963. Baboon ecology and human evolution. In *African Ecology and Human Evolution,* edited by F. C. Howell and F. Bourliére, pp. 335–67.

Elkisch, P. 1945. Children's drawings in a projective technique. *Psychological Monographs* 58(1):1–31.

Erikson, E. H. 1963. *Childhood and Society.* 2nd ed. New York: Norton.

———. 1975. *Life History and the Historical Moment.* New York: Wiley.

Freedman, D. G. 1968a. An evolutionary framework for behavioral research. In *Progress in Human Behavior Genetics,* edited by S. G. Vandenberg, pp. 1–5. Baltimore: Johns Hopkins Press.

———. 1968b. Personality development in infancy: a biological approach. In *Perspectives in Human Evolution,* edited by S. Washburn, vol. 1, pp. 258–87. New York: Holt, Rinehart & Winston.

———. 1971. Genetic influences on development of behavior. In *Normal and Abnormal Development of Brain and Behaviour,* edited by G. B. A. Stoelinga and J. J. van der Werff ten Bosch, pp. 208–33. Leiden: Leiden University Press.

———. 1974. *Human Infancy: An Evolutionary Perspective.* New York: Wiley (Halsted).

———. 1975. The development of social hierarchies. In *Society, Stress and Disease,* vol. 2, edited by L. Levi, pp. 36–42. London: Oxford University Press.

———. 1976. Infancy, biology, and culture. In *Developmental Psychobiology,* edited by L. R. Lipsitt, pp. 35–54. Hillsdale, N.J.: Erlbaum.

———. 1979. *Human Sociobiology.* New York: Free Press.

Freedman, D. G., and Freedman, N. 1969. Behavioural differences between Chinese-American and European-American newborns. *Nature* 224:1227.

Freedman, D. G., Loring, C. B., and Martin, R. M. 1967. Emotional behavior and personality development. In *Infancy and Early Childhood: A Handbook and Guide to Human Development,* edited by Y. Brackbill, pp. 429–502. New York: Free Press.

Freeman, B. J., Ritvo, E. R., Yokota, A., and Ritvo, A. 1986. A scale for rating symptoms of patients with the syndrome of autism in real life settings. *Journal of the American Academy of Child Psychiatry* 25(1):130–36.

Garai, J. E., and Scheinfeld, A. 1968. Sex differences in mental and behavioral traits. *Genetic Psychology Monographs* 77:169–299.

Goldstein, K. 1940. *Human Nature in the Light of Psychopathology.* Cambridge, Mass.: Harvard University Press.

———. 1957. The smiling of the infant and the problem of understanding the "other." *Journal of Psychology* 44:175–91.

Goodenough, F. L. 1926. *Measurement of Intelligence by Drawing.* Yonkers, N.Y.: World Book Co.

Harris, D. B. 1963. *Children's Drawings as Measures of Intellect and Maturity: A Revision and Extension of the Goodenough Draw-a-Man Test.* New York: Harcourt, Brace & World.

Kaila, E. 1932. Die Reaktionen des Säuglings auf das menschliche Gesicht [The reactions of the infant to the human face]. *Annales Universitatis Aboensis,* B ser., 17:1–114.

Kanner, L. 1949. Problems of nosology and psychodynamics of early infantile autism. *American Journal of Orthopsychiatry* 19:416–26.

———. 1954. To what extent is early infantile autism determined by constitutional inadequacies? *Research Publication of the Association for Research in Nervous and Mental Disease* 33:378–85.

Klages, L. 1923. *Ausdrucksbewegung und Gestaltungskraft [Gesture and Creation],* 3rd and 4th ed. Leipzig: Barth.

Koppitz, E. M. 1968. *Psychological Evaluation of Children's Human Figure Drawings.* New York: Grune & Stratton.

Leventhal, Bennett, L., February 1983. Interview with author. Chicago, Illinois.

Lewis, M., Kagan, J., and Kalafat, J. 1966. Patterns of fixation in the young infant. *Child Development* 37:331–41.

Machover, K. 1949. *Personality Projection in the Drawing of the Human Figure.* Springfield, Ill.: Thomas.

McLean, J. D. 1970. "Sex-Correlated Differences in Human Smiling Behavior: A Preliminary Investigation." Manuscript, Committee on Human Development, University of Chicago.

Mead, M. 1939. *From the South Seas: Studies of Adolescence and Sex in Primitive Societies.* New York: Morrow.

Morris, D. 1962. *The Biology of Art.* New York: Knopf.

Munroe, R. L., and Munroe, R. H. 1975. *Cross-Cultural Human Development.* Monterey, Calif.: Brooks/Cole.

Omark, D. R., and Edelman, M. S. 1973. "Peer Group Formation in Young Children; I. Action. II. Perception." Ph.D. diss., Committee on Human Development, University of Chicago.

Omark, D. R., Omark, M., and Edelman, M. S. 1975. Formation of dominance hierarchies in young children: action and perception. In *Psychological Anthropology*, edited by T. R. Williams, pp. 289–315. The Hague: Mouton. (Paper presented at the IXth International Congress of Anthropological and Ethnological Sciences, Chicago, 1973.)

Piaget, J. [1947] 1950. *The Psychology of Intelligence*. Translated by M. Percy and D. E. Berlyne. London: Routledge & Kegan Paul. (Original work published in 1947 as *La psychologie de l'intelligence*. A. Colin, Paris.)

———. [1936] 1952. *The Origins of Intelligence in Children*. Translated by M. Cook. New York: International Universities Press. (Original work published in 1936 as *La naissance de l'intelligence chez l'enfant*. Delachaux & Niestlé, Neuchâtel.)

———. [1937] 1954. *The Construction of Reality in the Child*. Translated by M. Cook. New York: Basic Books. (Original work published in 1937 as *La construction du réel chez l'enfant*. Delachaux & Niestlé, Neuchâtel.)

Piaget, J., and Inhelder, B. [1966] 1969. *The Psychology of the Child*. Translated by H. Weaver. New York: Basic Books. (Original work published in 1966 as *La psychologie de l'enfant*. Presses Universitaires de France, Paris.)

Prinzhorn, H. 1923. *Bildnerei der Geisteskranken: Ein Beitrag zur Psychologie und Psychopathologie der Gestaltung [Drawing of the Mentally Ill: On the Psychology and Psychopathology of Design]*, 2nd ed. Berlin: Verlag Julius Springer.

Rebelsky, F., and Daniel, P. 1976. Cross-cultural studies of infant intelligence. In *Origins of Intelligence*, edited by M. Lewis, pp. 279–97. New York: Plenum.

Rimland, B. 1964. *Infantile Autism: The Syndrome and Its Implications for a Neural Theory of Behavior*. Englewood Cliffs, N.J.: Prentice-Hall.

———. 1968. On the objective diagnosis of infantile autism. *Acta Paedopsychiatrica* 35:146–61.

———. 1978 (August). Inside the mind of the autistic savant. *Psychology Today* 12(3):68–80.

Ritvo, E. R., and Freeman, B. J. 1978. The national society for autistic children's definition of the syndrome of autism. *Journal of the American Academy of Child Psychiatry* 17(4):565–76.

Ritvo, E. R., Freeman, B. J., Yuwiler, A., Geller, E., Schroth, P., Yokota, A., Mason-Brothers, A., August, G. J., Klykylo, W., Leventhal, B. L., Lewis, K., Piggott, L. E., Realmuto, G., Stubbs, E. G., and Umansky, R. 1986. Fenfluramine treatment of autism: UCLA-collaborative study of 81 patients at 9 medical centers. *Psychopharmacology Bulletin* 22(1):133–40.

Scarr-Salapatek, S. 1976. An evolutionary perspective on infant intelligence: species patterns and individual variations. In *Origins of Intelligence,* edited by M. Lewis, pp. 165–97. New York: Plenum.

Seifert, C. D. 1990*a*. *Theories of Autism*. Lanham, Md.: University Press of America.

———. 1990*b*. *Case Studies in Autism: A Young Child and Two Adolescents*. Lanham, Md.: University Press of America.

Stevens, C. 1972. "An Ethological Investigation of Social Interaction Among Third Graders." Master's thesis, Committee on Human Development, University of Chicago.

Strumpfer, D. J. W. 1963. The relation of Draw-a-Person test variables to age and chronicity in psychotic groups. *Journal of Clinical Psychology* 19:208–11.

Swensen, C. H. 1955. Sexual differentiation on the Draw-a-Person test. *Journal of Clinical Psychology* 11:37–40.

———. 1968. Empirical evaluation of human figure drawings: 1957–1966. *Psychological Bulletin* 70:20–44.

Thomas, A., and Chess, S. 1977. *Temperament and Development*. New York: Brunner/Mazel.

The Author

Cheryl D. Seifert trained in pediatric psychology at The University of Chicago, Wyler Children's Hospital, Department of Pediatrics, Pediatric Mental Development Clinic, Joseph P. Kennedy, Jr., Mental Retardation Center, and specialized in mental development and retardation. She held staff positions at The University of Chicago, Wyler Children's Hospital, Department of Pediatrics, Pediatric Psychological Services; Michael Reese Hospital and Medical Center, Dysfunctioning Child Center; and Mount Sinai Hospital Medical Center of Chicago, Department of Pediatrics, Pediatric Ecology Program.

She is the author of *Theories of Autism* and *Case Studies in Autism: A Young Child and Two Adolescents.*